This book
Belongs to

_____

_____

A2 Irregular Verbs

Base form	Past Simple	Past Participle
be	was/were	been
begin	began	begun
break	broke	broken
bring	brought	brought
build	built	built
buy	bought	bought
catch	caught	caught
come	came	come
cost	cost	cost
cut	cut	cut
do	did	done
draw	drew	drawn
drink	drank	drunk
eat	ate	eaten
fall	fell	fallen
find	found	found
fly	flew	flown
forget	forgot	forgotten
get	got	got
give	gave	given
go	went	gone
have	had	had
hear	heard	heard
hit	hit	hit
hold	held	held
hurt	hurt	hurt
keep	kept	kept

A2 Irregular Verbs

Base form	Past Simple	Past Participle
know	knew	known
learn	learnt/learned	learnt/learned
leave	left	left
mean	meant	meant
meet	met	met
put	put	put
read	read	read
ring	rang	rung
run	ran	run
say	said	said
see	saw	seen
show	showed	shown
shut	shut	shut
sit	sat	sat
sleep	slept	slept
speak	spoke	spoken
spend	spent	spent
stand	stood	stood
steal	stole	stolen
swim	swam	swum
take	took	taken
teach	taught	taught
tell	told	told
think	thought	thought
understand	understood	understood
win	won	won
write	wrote	written

FACE PARTS

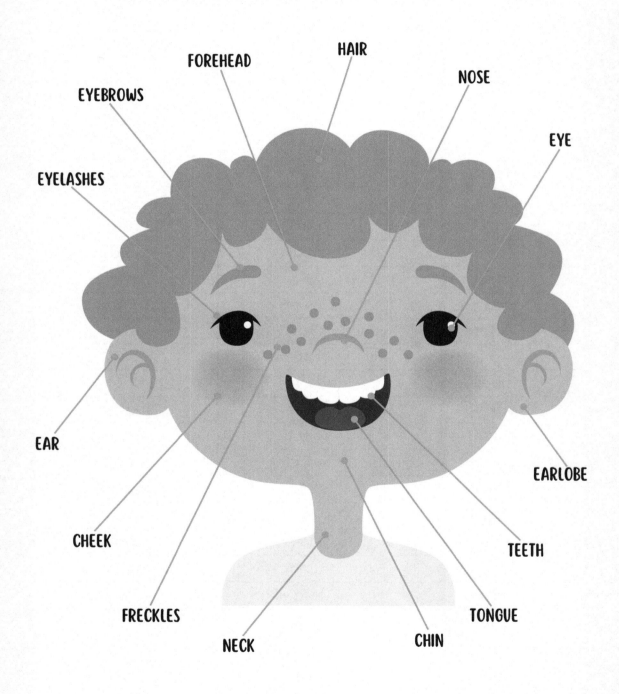

FOREHEAD

HAIR

NOSE

EYEBROWS

EYE

EYELASHES

EAR

EARLOBE

CHEEK

TEETH

FRECKLES

TONGUE

NECK

CHIN

IT IS A GOOD DAY TO LEARN FACE PARTS.

CLASSROOM OBJECTS

test tube	globe	compass	bag
scissors	calculator	paintbrush	protractor
pallete	pencil	book	pen

ENGLISH ALPHABET

Aa
apple

Bb
ball

Cc
cat

Dd
duck

Ee
egg
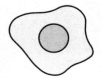

Ff
flower

Gg
grape

Hh
hat

Ii
igloo
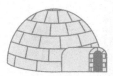

Jj
jam

Kk
kite

Ll
lion

Mm
monkey

Nn
nose

Oo
owl

Pp
pig

Qq
Queen

Rr
rose

Ss
sun

Tt
tiger

Uu
umbrella

Vv
violin

Ww
water

Xx
xylophone

Yy
yoyo

Zz
zipper

ANIMALS
ALPHABET POSTER

Jobs and Occupations

A VET

A STEWARDESS

A SINGER

AN ARCHAELOGIST

A DOCTOR

AN ENGINEER

A DANCER

A TEACHER

A FIREFIGHTER

AN ARTIST

AN ASTRONAUT

A POLICEMAN

Feelings & Emotions

PROUD

BORED

CURIOUS

PLAYFUL

TIRED

HUNGRY

ANGRY

WORRIED

SCARED

HAPPY

CONFUSED

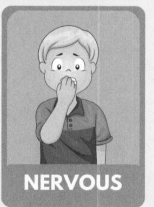
NERVOUS

DISGUSTED

ANNOYED

SAD

AMUSED

Vegetables

potato

eggplant

carrot

cucumber

pumpkin

chard

ginger

peas

beet

cauliflower

zucchini

broccoli

Vegetables

radish

spinach

leek

turnip

chili

lettuce

celery

onion

garlic

kale

cabbage

bell pepper

Words for the Weather

Sunny

Windy

Cloudy

Rainy

Snowy

Sunny

Windy

Cloudy

Snowy

Autumn

Spring

Summer

Winter

ADDITION

combine	add
sum	plus
join	more
and	increase
total	altogether

SUBTRACTION

less	fewer
leave	reduce
minus	remain
subtract	decrease
difference	take away

MULTIPLICATION

times

factors

lots of

groups of

product

DIVISION

share

sharing

equal groups

grouping

share equally

WORD	PLURAL	OPPOSITE	MEANING

SENTENCES AND EXPRESSIONS

WORD	PLURAL	OPPOSITE	MEANING

SENTENCES AND EXPRESSIONS

WORD	PLURAL	OPPOSITE	MEANING

WORD	PLURAL	OPPOSITE	MEANING

SENTENCES AND EXPRESSIONS

WORD	PLURAL	OPPOSITE	MEANING

SENTENCES AND EXPRESSIONS

WORD	PLURAL	OPPOSITE	MEANING

SENTENCES AND EXPRESSIONS

WORD	PLURAL	OPPOSITE	MEANING

SENTENCES AND EXPRESSIONS

WORD	PLURAL	OPPOSITE	MEANING

SENTENCES AND EXPRESSIONS

WORD	PLURAL	OPPOSITE	MEANING

SENTENCES AND EXPRESSIONS

WORD	PLURAL	OPPOSITE	MEANING

SENTENCES AND EXPRESSIONS

WORD	PLURAL	OPPOSITE	MEANING

SENTENCES AND EXPRESSIONS

WORD	PLURAL	OPPOSITE	MEANING

SENTENCES AND EXPRESSIONS

WORD	PLURAL	OPPOSITE	MEANING

SENTENCES AND EXPRESSIONS

WORD	PLURAL	OPPOSITE	MEANING

SENTENCES AND EXPRESSIONS

WORD	PLURAL	OPPOSITE	MEANING

SENTENCES AND EXPRESSIONS

WORD	PLURAL	OPPOSITE	MEANING

SENTENCES AND EXPRESSIONS

WORD	PLURAL	OPPOSITE	MEANING

SENTENCES AND EXPRESSIONS

WORD	PLURAL	OPPOSITE	MEANING

SENTENCES AND EXPRESSIONS

WORD	PLURAL	OPPOSITE	MEANING

SENTENCES AND EXPRESSIONS

WORD	PLURAL	OPPOSITE	MEANING

SENTENCES AND EXPRESSIONS

WORD	PLURAL	OPPOSITE	MEANING

SENTENCES AND EXPRESSIONS

WORD	PLURAL	OPPOSITE	MEANING

SENTENCES AND EXPRESSIONS

WORD	PLURAL	OPPOSITE	MEANING

SENTENCES AND EXPRESSIONS

WORD	PLURAL	OPPOSITE	MEANING

SENTENCES AND EXPRESSIONS

WORD	PLURAL	OPPOSITE	MEANING

SENTENCES AND EXPRESSIONS

WORD	PLURAL	OPPOSITE	MEANING

SENTENCES AND EXPRESSIONS

WORD	PLURAL	OPPOSITE	MEANING

SENTENCES AND EXPRESSIONS

WORD	PLURAL	OPPOSITE	MEANING

SENTENCES AND EXPRESSIONS

WORD	PLURAL	OPPOSITE	MEANING

SENTENCES AND EXPRESSIONS

WORD	PLURAL	OPPOSITE	MEANING

SENTENCES AND EXPRESSIONS

WORD	PLURAL	OPPOSITE	MEANING

SENTENCES AND EXPRESSIONS

WORD	PLURAL	OPPOSITE	MEANING

SENTENCES AND EXPRESSIONS

WORD	PLURAL	OPPOSITE	MEANING

SENTENCES AND EXPRESSIONS

WORD	PLURAL	OPPOSITE	MEANING

SENTENCES AND EXPRESSIONS

WORD	PLURAL	OPPOSITE	MEANING

SENTENCES AND EXPRESSIONS

WORD	PLURAL	OPPOSITE	MEANING

SENTENCES AND EXPRESSIONS

WORD	PLURAL	OPPOSITE	MEANING

SENTENCES AND EXPRESSIONS

WORD	PLURAL	OPPOSITE	MEANING

SENTENCES AND EXPRESSIONS

WORD	PLURAL	OPPOSITE	MEANING

SENTENCES AND EXPRESSIONS

WORD	PLURAL	OPPOSITE	MEANING

SENTENCES AND EXPRESSIONS

The Weather

It's sunny

It's cloudy

It's rainy

It's stormy

It's windy

HOW TO LEARN ENGLISH

BUILD YOUR VOCABULARY

Work on building your vocabulary every day by choosing new words to learn and repeating each word over and over to reinforce the memory of those new words.

SPEAK ENGLISH

Speaking English daily will help your confidence while speaking the language. Keep in mind that confidence is the key to sounding natural.

ACTIVE LISTENING

Listen intently to a variety of English content anywhere you can. Paying close attention to sources like the news, popular songs and everyday conversations can greatly increase your knowledge of words and expressions.

PRACTICE WITH FRIENDS

Set up scenarios with friends so you can role play in different settings to practice your new vocabulary and phrases. Since you won't know what your friend will say next, it's great practice for thinking quickly.

SET GOALS

Setting goals and rewards is a fun way to reinforce your learning and to celebrate each achievement you make along the way. New languages are always difficult, but with practice you will be a pro in no time.

SPELLING TIC TAC TOE

Practice new words choosing and completing 3 activities in a row.

Write the words in **bubble** letters	Write the words 3 times each	Rainbow write the words
Write your words in alphabetical order	Write the words with capital letters	Write the words in cursive letters
Write your words and draw them	Write each word in a sentence	B BL BLU BLUE Write each word in a pyramid

5 USEFUL TIPS
TO GET INTERNATIONAL SCHOLARSHIP

1 IMPROVE YOUR ENGLISH SKILL

You can start by frequently memorizing English vocabulary with tutoring and taking the TOEFL test. However, don't be lazy to hone your skills in English consistently. If necessary, take the time to take a special package to learn English. That way, you will quickly master it.

2 WRITE A GOOD MOTIVATION LETTER

Try to write down some interesting things, such as you are very interested in the country because you often watch some of its films, you have friends who live there, or you have high school friends who have participated in student exchanges in that country. That shows that you do have a strong desire and foundation.

3 CHOOSE A COUNTRY WITH FEW RIVALS

This method can be said to be quite effective in getting scholarships abroad. If you want to be a little different from the average person, you have a greater chance of getting a scholarship.

4 PREPARE A LETTER OF RECOMMENDATION

Letters of recommendation play an important role in the scholarship process. Because the letter contains that you deserve to get a scholarship from the institution that provides it, to get a letter of recommendation, try to ask your teacher, extracurricular coach, or guardian for references.

5 PREPARE A PORTFOLIO

You can prepare a portfolio and CV as a condition for getting a scholarship. In addition, a good portfolio and CV packaging can impact results. Therefore, it's a good idea to package your data as neatly as possible so the organizers can get complete information about you. But more importantly, try to keep your portfolio relevant to the major you're after

More Information to Study Adboard

@reallygreatsite   www.reallygreatsite.com   hello@reallygreatsite.com

MONTHS OF THE YEAR

January	July
February	August
March	September
April	October
May	November
June	December

Printed in Great Britain
by Amazon

39194031R00064